# 25 STAGES OF MY SPINE

# 25 stages
# of my spine

# Margaret Randall

The Elizabeth Press
New Rochelle, N.Y.

© Copyright 1967, The Elizabeth Press

Publisher's acknowledgement: this poem, in an earlier version, appeared originally in *El Corno Emplumado* under the title "The Molecules".

Printed at the Press of Villiers Publications Ltd.
Ingestre Road, London, NW5, England

this book, for Sergio

1.

*begins . . .*

each part the trees
the self which is made
and put forth
i live as a group a combine
the whole those pieces form
and sing
the same note being still as clear
transparent hot or sounding
as that dog's whistle
beyond the ear where each part

it is true it couldn't be less whole
in pieces

2.

*sergio* . . .

at your feet as they go out
just at that very opening
one moves apart
from the other
still
comes back
reaches forward and again forward
the continuous animal

just at your very feet as they go
lifting the shadow
on a day like that
held by the heel of your shoe
sucked between your legs

as you go

3.

*sergio . . .*

after you have said it twice
for emphasis
marking the words with a red pencil
looking at my face
to assure the register you say
don't
take it so seriously don't
you remember
my preface my warning
one must be

logical
and die

4.


*sergio . . .*

when you slam the door and say
ditto
i can't sleep here
why did you pull the damn cord so hard
will go to the studio
bang
the silence cuts
skin stretched
by tooth and finger my body
grows black in to out and then

you open the door come back in
silent      still
screwdriver and pliers in hand

no words

5.

*the others . . .*

the big blue coat and gold buttons
though tarnished
surrounding meat
flesh
ragged sweater hanging from one hand
says
he hit me hard got away
and

twelve men both sides of eternal fence
9th precinct mexico city
fill the room

long bellylaugh

6.

*myself* . . .

it is here i say here
where i hurt
blue wine for vintage and
a case for questions

the child's finger
points to tummy tooth or head
and mine

to hapless air

7.

*and that, too . . .*

the daily press instructed
makes a case for johnson's trip
big daddy
from the north
he stretches his hand in clenched fist
the workers

get the day off are paid
in truckloads
they come waving little flags
through wine and caviar the american ambassador
plays his trombone
and ladybird sings guadalajara

o guadalajara
memories of honeymoon
and little mexican children
taught once by the big man
in texas
where mexicans and dogs are not let in
to certain places
houses ranchstyle oil wells or
telephone booths
his hand on the phone

a private line
his hand on the phone the busy signal says
the line is dead

8.

*the books . . .*

from eight flowers
i choose four
it's more than half

artaud is dead but killed the cabbala
before he went

9.

*sergio . . .*

my mouth feels sometimes
in the jean moreau movie i am still moving
my mouth moves around the edges
under the skin the smile
that particular smile

in stages

i would like you to say
how can a mouth be that perfect
especially this lip pointing to
caressing
the upper

but mine speaks a different harsher language
is filled with foreign logic
reaches

nonetheless for the offering
a tenderness

tongue gone now

only tooth

10.


*the little children who lead us . . .*

i see again
what fenollosa saw
as he my child

writes

from fingers forms letters copies smiles
the letters the words
have their own intention
form

it does not go
according to alphabet or ruler
but up and down

with spring's design

11.


*moving about/against us . . .*

what will we say to them what will
we give them
on that plate
when they hand it out
out

what goes there
is put inside those bellies

a poem?

**12.**

*robert creeley* . . .

those trees
are curious but then
we only see

what grows above the ground

13.


*the dream, in space . . .*

i lie down
on that corn altar
growing out of my eyes the ears
from between the toes of my feet
and hands
the corn
as instrument
feelers jumping to a static call
from my hands from the stages of my spine

the knobs bent
coiled
corn     a rope     that altar
husks ripening as hearts
offered up
cut out and offered up
only

the altar remains
and i from years
laid out on it

**14.**

*chambers* . . .

judith
what surrounds
chambers close in i wait
the pulse of it is long
and tedious
reacts recharged against

my limbs
the limit of the line

and breath

15.


*help from a professional . . .*

this is not indifference he says
but fear

the leaning in between
a going out and coming back

a hundred times in one minute
how

to measure it

16.


*bill truesdale . . .*

what can i say
of those old poems
showing

with curved smile
what can i tell discover

the shame gives place to growth
a growing

upward or downward or
outward even

 :remember

**17.**

*the act of it . . .*

plant
a lip in the soil
of my face
head
a fine flower or cactus with
one bloom

it bursts at morning
grows hot in sun
the color ripens fades is dead

by dark

18.

*ximena* . . .

the youngest
raised by habit love disregard or
indolence

walks runs pushes that energy
tremendous
forward

cries or laughs alot
moves
along repeated line

then softly
 :papa
to me or him or both
repeated

her own ecstasy

19.

*minutes . . .*

hunger is
more than pain a reaching out
around

the unfilled space

not there

20.

*hours* . . .

those words do not go
with the expression on your face
rather
not a mask even but

the elements
from which a music
more than twelve tones

uncountable in that cold measure

21.

*weeks . . .*

if you want
need
more than that you must reach

a door where opening
the cold air

comes from inside the room

22.

*george and angela bowering* . . .

in silence they wait and
in silence they fall and
in silence

no one hears the name
unsaid    used    cutting

through the lip
swollen
in silence

23.

*jerome rothenberg* . . .

a calm door a calm way
to go through
calmly

a very calm entrance

into a calm place
very stitched
slowly and calmly

no wind by man
by man or element
no wind calmly

no wind by no man
by no element
calmly

an entrance with
no wind
into not heard calmly

and with patience
to wait
calmly into

**24.**

*alvin greenberg . . .*

there is a part of this
the part called risk
gets into me
i break it apart with my hands
examine

what of it touches me
calls
what thumbprint or tracing
it leaves on shoulders
along spine or
afterwards

this wistful item telling
this that is most there
discovering
comes out from in itself
breaks me
in light and highstrung pieces

electric
like the way a water runs
or stops

in sand

25.


*sergio* . . . . .

and to say i love you
like flowerpots
the filling stands aside
is only what covers what goes
around it

words a blanket
or roof
walls already mossing
better to say

come
be with me here
run your feet in time with mine
my own with yours
come
sit on this honeycomb

of firelight
and fists
corners and waves of loose warm air
catching us
putting us where
our own reflection

speaks to us